KOREA:
FROZEN HELL ON EARTH

A Platoon Sergeant's Diary
Korean War 1950-1951

BORIS R. SPIROFF

1SG-E8 USA (RET.)

American Literary Press, Inc.
Five Star Special Edition
Baltimore, Maryland

KOREA: FROZEN HELL ON EARTH
A Platoon Sergeant's diary
Korean War 1950-1951

Copyright © 1998 Boris R. Spiroff

Library of Congress
Cataloging in Publication Data
ISBN 1-56167-425-7

Library of Congress Card Catalog Number:
98-84298

Published by

American Literary Press, Inc.
Five Star Special Edition
8019 Belair Road, Suite 10
Baltimore, Maryland 21236

Manufactured in the United States of America

Dedication

To my beloved wife, Cassie, whose unending love, affection, and encouragement gave me the inspiration, the hope, and the strength to carry on, to face and overcome each and every obstacle and adverse condition.

Also, with her retention of all my letters from Korea containing vital information in regard to the date, time, and the weather of each occurrence, this book would not have been possible.

Table of Contents

Preface

This book is intended to summarize my personal experiences and involvement in the Korean Conflict. I do not mean to indulge in the policies and/or politics between the Republic of Korea (ROK) and her neighboring nations, whose disagreements eventually brought on the war. The facts regarding how and why this war occurred are fully explained in various books regarding Korea's stormy history. Though I mention other American units throughout the book, including the ROK Army and the various UN forces who were, at times, on line with us, my primary concern deals with the actions of my assigned unit, namely Company G, Second Battalion of the Seventh Calvary Regiment. I was not, nor were any other noncommissioned officers to my knowledge, privy to the "big picture" regarding our status, or to the overall tactical operations. All strategies, tactical operations, and unit missions originated at the Supreme United Nations Command from where they were delegated to the fighting units.

Insofar as specific objectives, missions, battles, and the results of each that I mention occurring on various dates and times are concerned, the information was gathered and obtained from the frequent critiques, briefings, and the unit's objectives furnished to the platoon sergeants and platoon leaders by our company commander. The contents herein regarding my personal involvement were obtained from my own (and very incomplete) diary, from letters I had written to my wife, which she kept on file by dates received (which did not necessarily correspond to the order in which they were written due to the inevitable delivery problems), and primarily from the previously mentioned company commander's critiques and briefings. Although I seldom mention the activity of the company commander or the platoon leader, except when the occasion requires, nothing was ever done nor any action taken without their knowledge or approval, except in situations when neither was available due to the circumstances.

I had intended to write this book several times previously, but I kept putting it off. I found it difficult to relive and relay on paper all the misery, hardship, and frustration endured during the war by everyone there. However, after forty-three years, there seems to be a deja -vu. Ashes are being rekindled and flames are being fanned. Trouble is again brewing between the two Koreas. The United States is again concerned with North Korea's aggression. Therefore, I believe it is only fitting and proper to relate what transpired there from 1950 through 1953.

Though my intent in writing this book is to relate to the reader my own personal experiences, I want to mention that the extreme cold weather, the bitter cold winds, the deep and icy snows, the slippery muddy fields caused by the heavy summer rains, the high and rocky mountainous ridges and last but not least the sickening smell of human excrement used to fertilize the numerous rice paddies, will forever be remembered by every foot soldier, every infantryman, and every marine who served in Korea.

Though this book is about the thirteen months I spent in Korea, it is not about me. I have, however, attempted to give an account of the daily events of my unit's involvement as they occurred and as I witnessed them. It is primarily about the many trials and tribulations, hardships and heartaches, hazards and discomforts and frequent disappointments endured by gallant American soldiers, and of their amazing ability to endure the adversity of a bloody, cruel, and miserable war. The book is not about individual accomplishments or heroes, rather about a group of men performing a thankless duty against great odds for a given time. For many of them, time ran out. The events described herein of friends and fellow soldiers who made the full and final sacrifice had to be told. We cannot let this war remain as the FORGOTTEN WAR!

Prelude to Korea (1937 - 1949)

I entered the Service in 1937 from Baltimore, Maryland, one day after my seventeenth birthday. Enlisting in the United States Army, I was assigned to the Fourteenth Infantry Regiment, Canal Zone, Panama. After my second tour there, I was due to return home in March 1942. However, with the war raging in Europe and Japan attacking Pearl Harbor on December 7, 1941, all discharges were "frozen" for the duration of the war.

I remained in Panama until March 1943, attaining the rank of staff sergeant. At this time, as a member of a cadre, I returned to the States, arriving at Camp Livingstone, Louisiana. This was a holding area for troops destined for overseas assignments. Our group or cadre was composed of sufficient critical personnel and noncommissioned officers needed to form a regimental size unit capable of jungle warfare. We were destined for the Pacific theater.

This, however, never materialized for me and several others. Due to our knowledge of a foreign language, we were interviewed and eventually selected by the newly formed Special Forces organization, namely the Office of Strategic Services, better known as OSS. Our mission was to join and operate with partisan (guerrilla) forces waging warfare against the German troops occupying their homeland. In my particular case the country was Yugoslavia. I was among the 250 officers, noncommissioned officers, and enlisted men, the initial portion of the 2671st Special Recon Battalion, under the command of Major John Urban, who arrived there on January 4, 1944. Our base of operations was the Island of Vis, one of the Dalmatian Islands (off the coast of Yugoslavia) not occupied by German troops. Periodic surprise raids from Vis on these islands by partisan troops, accompanied by OSS patrols and at times by British commandos, forced the Germans to evacuate, liberating the islands.

One memorable occasion remains vivid. It took place on the Island of Hvar between February 20 and March 1, 1944. Captain Andy Rogers with a party of seven, including a Yugoslav guide and me as an interpreter, was dropped off there for reconnaissance purposes. Our mission was to determine the number of German troops stationed on the island, were they were quartered, how and when they received supplies, their activities, and the type of patrol they normally used.

On the night of February 24, on a narrow street leading to the waterfront, we came face to face with an eight-man German patrol. Our meeting resulted in a close-quarters shoot out. After the exchange of fire, lasting less than one minute, six Germans had been killed and two wounded. We had one man wounded. Sergeant Jimmy Zevitas, who was in line behind me, was shot near the groin. We evaded the German search parties with their dogs for two days until finally being picked up by British commandos in motorboats.

For this action I was awarded the Bronze Star, recommended by Captain Rogers.

Later that year, on September 2, 1944, an advance reconnaissance party, consisting of Lieutenant Jack McConnell, myself, and four others, made a night parachute jump into the mainland, landing near Mostar in Bosnia. By prearrangement, we were met by a group of partisans, part of Marshal Tito's Nineteenth Brigade, and we proceeded with our mission. Our primary objective was to harass the German convoys who were evacuating Greece and heading for Germany. We did this by mining the roads at critical locations thus halting their convoys. They were then sitting ducks, as we would machine-gun them from the hills. We instructed the partisans how to fire American mortars, bazookas, and the fifty caliber machine guns. To summarize my Yugoslav involvement, the OSS mission there was successfully terminated in October 1944.

Our team was withdrawn to Bari, Italy, home base for OSS headquarters, where the "Cloak and Dagger Club" originated. From there we were subsequently reassigned to other front line units, some in Italy and some in France. I arrived at the Thirteenth Airborne Division in southern France in January 1945. At this time the Allied forces seized the offensive, driving the Germans out of France. The tide was turned. American airborne units from France invaded Germany, dropping by parachute across the Rhine River. This surprise attack coupled with Germany having lost the Battle of the Bulge, hastened her surrender. Following Adolph Hitler's suicide on April 30, 1945, Germany surrendered unconditionally on May 8, 1945 (V.E. Day).

With the war in Europe finished, I, among others, was returned to the States. We arrived at Fort George G. Meade, Maryland in July 1945. I was given a thirty-day furlough, after which I would be assigned to an OSS unit in Burma. Unlike Germany, Japan had not surrendered. Bitter fighting continuing throughout the Pacific theater.

During the course of my furlough, an atomic bomb was dropped on the city of Hiroshima on August 6, 1945. A second bomb was dropped on the city of Nagasaki on August 9, hastening Japan's surrender. Japan finally surrendered unconditionally on August 14, 1945, thus ending World War II, surely another "war to end all wars!"

Due to Japan's surrender, all orders for overseas assignments were canceled. I was discharged from the army with eight years of service and was assigned to the

Ready Reserve, stationed in Baltimore. Between 1945 and 1948, while still in the Reserve, I had several jobs, the final one as a shipping clerk for Railway Express. Prior to this I had applied for the Maryland State Police, but was rejected for being only five feet eight inches tall. The minimum requirement was five feet ten inches.

During early summer of 1948, due to the railroad's slack in business, a three month furlough was imposed on those most recently hired. This meant that I would be unemployed for most of the summer. At this time I received a letter from Maryland Military District stating that an honor guard/firing squad was being proposed for burial honors for the remains of the servicemen killed during the war. The squad was to be composed of reserve members for a three month duration. A new squad would be formed every three months until all the remains were returned. Being furloughed from Railway Express, I responded, as did thirty-three other reservists. Having a rank of tech sergeant, now known as sergeant first class, I was the senior member, hence I was appointed as squad leader. I had two weeks to select the twelve best men of the group, then form and train them into a formidable firing squad. This was no easy task, since I was not familiar with the personnel or their capabilities. Nevertheless, the task was accomplished, and after two weeks Captain Sickler was presented with a very fine firing squad.

Burial ceremonies averaged three or four a day at various cemeteries. The squad began receiving praises, acclamations, and commendations from various sources, particularly from VFW organizations attending the funerals. As a result, a decision was reached by Maryland Military District to retain the squad for the duration of the project instead of the three month period as previously planned. Finally, after eighteen months, with most of the remains returned, the squad was dissolved. All members, except myself, returned to their previous civilian status. I chose to return to the army, enlisting in the Third Armored

Cavalry Regiment at Fort George G. Meade, Maryland. In October 1949, I was appointed platoon sergeant of the Third Platoon of Company C.

Finally being stationed close to home, and not anticipating further assignment away from home for some time, I decided that now was a good time to get married. I had met my fiancee, Cassie, a nineteen-year old beauty of German descent with hazel eyes and brown hair, in October 1943, just prior to sailing for Europe. We both were in favor of waiting for the right time and situation before setting a wedding date. This seemed to be the time.

Meanwhile, things were not looking too good globally. There was much unrest and uprising everywhere. Korea seemed to be principally in the news, and communism was beginning to flaunt its influence throughout. This was a major concern to the United States, for it conflicted with President Truman's "Containment Doctrine," which he inaugurated in 1947. The doctrine's purpose was to contain and hold the line against communism's spread. This was the beginning of the infamous cold war, primarily between the United States and Russia.

Though the postwar years prior to 1950 were mostly serene, quiet, and somewhat peaceful, the year 1950 would prove to be quite turbulent. The United States would be involved in the problems of a troublesome country whose terrain and customs she was unfamiliar with and in a war for which she was unprepared.

Personal Highlights - 1950
Prior to Korea

January 7, 1950

On a clear, cold and blustery Saturday afternoon, Cassie and I were married. The wedding took place at St. John's Lutheran Church on Warwick Street near Frederick Avenue in southwest Baltimore. The maid of honor was Cassie's sister Helen, and the best man was David Manners, a member of my platoon. Though I was stationed in Fort Meade, we lived with Cassie's parents, John and Katherine Schnitzlein, in Linthicum, Maryland, near Fort Meade.

For the next few months, army duty, maneuvers, and other army requirements kept Cassie and me apart most of the time. In spite of all this, I considered these few months to be one of the happiest times of my life. Meanwhile, the constant bickering, accusations, and minor skirmishes between North and South Korea were worsening. News reports informed of North Korea's aggression and of its army build up along the Thirty-eighth parallel, which separates the two Koreas. The skirmishes and artillery duels between the two continued on through the month of May, causing more concern to the United States, primarily because of Soviet "advisers" within the North Korean army.

Between February and June regular army routine kept me extremely busy, especially in preparing for the annual

Inspector General's Inspection. With all of my previous service being in the Infantry and the OSS, learning armored technique was a chore and a challenge. Participating in maneuvers at Camp A. P. Hill, Virginia and traveling to other way out locations to instruct ROTC officers in weapons firing, kept me away from home. In addition, I attended classes on the proper method of loading heavy equipment and armored vehicles on transport planes. I also attended classes on the proper telephone and radio communication between tank commanders while in combat. I looked forward to and really appreciated the days and weekends when I had the opportunity to go home and spend some time with my wife.

January 7, 1950: Cassie and I were married.
Five months later I received my orders for Korea.

My Personal
Korean War Timetable

June 25-27, 1950

On June 25, 1950, the Communist forces of North Korea finally crossed the thirty-eighth parallel into South Korea, inflicting much damage and heavy casualties. This was the big news headline of the day. The United States was deeply concerned that this act has occurred, especially for the lives of the small number of American troops stationed there.

On June 27, President Truman ordered General Douglas MacArthur to leave Japan and report to Korea, appointing him commander of the United Nations forces in Korea. Things were beginning to warm up!

July 18, 1950

Company C and the entire First Battalion has been here at Bethany Beach, Delaware, for the past two days instructing ROTC officers how to fire 60 and 90 millimeter artillery. Today, July 18, I was instructed to report to battalion headquarters. Arriving there, I was handed a special notice by the battalion commander, signed by President Truman, stating that due to my military specialty (Infantry MOS) and my World War II experience, my presence was needed in Korea as soon as possible. Though disappointed at the notice, I was not surprised due to what is occurring in Korea. Being a regular army, career soldier, I sort of expected it sooner or later. My only regret is that I was only recently married. I know that this will be a great shock to Cassie, and I wonder how the news will affect her.

Since the outbreak of the Korean War and our involvement in it, many trained, previous servicemen, especially noncommissioned officers have been affected. They were taken from home based army units and assigned to front line units in Korea.

[According to postwar statistics, approximately 20 percent of the soldiers who served in Korea were World War II veterans.]

July 19, 1950

Today I returned to Fort Meade from Bethany Beach and almost immediately began processing for shipment. I, along with ten others, were the first replacements from Fort Meade for Korea. Among this group was my platoon leader, Lieutenant Paar, and two other members from my platoon, Pfc. A. Morales and Pfc. J. Spivey. We have less than two weeks to complete our processing and be on our way. I still have not told Cassie of my orders.

July 22, 1950

Still processing. Today we received our required immunization shots. As difficult as it was, I had to inform Cassie. As expected, she was very disappointed and quite worried about me. She tried to be brave about it, telling me not to worry about her, that she would be okay.

According to the local newspaper, the *Sun*, the US Twenty-Fifth Infantry and the First Cavalry divisions arrived in Korea from Japan, their primary mission being to reinforce the outmanned UN forces guarding the approaches to Pusan and Taegu.

July 27, 1950

"D" Day has finally arrived, and how I hated to see it

come, though I knew it was coming. We are to depart Fort Meade today. I feel bad, not so much for my sake, but for Cassie's. I hate to leave her. After being married, we didn't get a chance to spend much time together. My train is to depart at 9:00 PM from Camden Station, destination being Camp Stoneman, California. This is a transit holding area for troops bound for Korea.

Our drive to Camden Station is quite somber, to say the least, as was the half hour prior to my departure. Boarding the train is bad enough, but saying "good-bye" to Cassie was one of the most difficult and most painful experiences of my life. I knew it would be like this. I can still visualize her standing on the platform trying to hold back her tears. I will never forget how she finally broke down and cried as the train pulled away. [This trip marked my first step toward the Korean hell!]

July 31, 1950

It's been four days since I left Baltimore. The trip was okay and pleasant, and it could have been enjoyable were it not for the reason I was making it. I finally arrived at Camp Stoneman at 12:30 PM by way of Chicago, Saint Louis, New Mexico, and other points west. The weather on arrival is very hot and dry. Camp Stoneman appears to be a typical army post, extremely hot and dry most of the summer and very cold and windy in the winter. The barracks remind me of Fort Meade.

Today I got acquainted with Sergeant First Class William Ford, a five-foot ten-inch, 170-pound, previous serviceman who seems to be very nice, good humored, friendly, and intelligent. He appears to be a very good soldier. [We would become the best of friends.]

During my stay at Camp Stoneman I am keeping in touch with Cassie through letters and by telephone. I'm certain that I am keeping both the telephone company and the post office in business. Cassie is keeping me informed of the news and conditions back home. Just hearing her voice is keeping up my morale.

August 7, 1950

The month of August just began with some very disheartening news from Korea. Today's news informs us that North Korean forces are marching on toward the port city, Pusan. American forces, primarily the Twenty-fifth Infantry Division, are being pushed back and suffering heavy casualties. Also, the First Cavalry Division, defending Taegu, is under attack by superior enemy troops, forcing them to give ground with many losses. Our men are in obvious grave and deep trouble.

Though Camp Stoneman is a typical army camp, I am getting use to it and will hate to leave here when the time comes. Especially when we read and hear of what is occurring in Korea. Today, August 7, is my brother Mike's birthday. I sent him a card and also called Cassie. She said that the weather in Baltimore is very hot. Hot or not, I'd like to be there right now.

September 8, 1950

We have been here at Camp Stoneman a little over five weeks. Finally the day of reckoning has arrived. We have just been told that we will be leaving after dinner, by plane, for Anchorage, Alaska. There we will refuel to continue on our flight to Korea.

September 9, 1950

Here we are at Anchorage, arriving here at 6:30 AM. We debarked from the plane expecting it to be cold and windy; however, it was not as cold as I expected it to be. But then, September is not one of the cold months. We had breakfast at the air base mess hall. The plane is being refueled and our departure time is 12:30 PM. I have a chance to write a letter to Cassie prior to take off.

We took off at 12:30 PM as scheduled, but after a few minutes in the air, we got the fright of our lives. The right engine caught fire, forcing us to return to the base. Fortunately, we landed safely. We will spend the night while repairs are made. Our next departure time will be at noon tomorrow. I wrote to Cassie telling her about our experience. [See letter dated September 9.]

September 10, 1950

As per schedule, we again departed at noon. Once again we received a scare. After a short flight smoke began coming from the same engine and we were forced to return to base. Luck was with us as we once again landed safely. The plane obviously needs major repairs. The officer in charge informed us that we will be leaving by a different plane when it arrives.

We have an opportunity to take in a part of Anchorage after which I will write some letters to Cassie and family. The weather today is not too bad. It gets colder as evening approaches. The Alaskan natives and some of the personnel stationed here consider the weather to be mild. I, however, find it to be sunny, clear, and quite a bit colder than I like it.

September 13, 1950

Today a plane arrived from the United States at 9:30 AM, bringing supplies to the air base and several troop replacements for Korea. These soldiers joined our group. Two of the men were from Fort Meade. It was decided that this plane will be used for our way overdue flight.

We departed shortly after 3:00 PM. No engine fire this time. We stopped at Kodiak Island to drop off mail and to refuel. This is an extremely cold and barren island with snow all around and a constant wind blowing. Kodiak is one of the chain of islands stretching west to southwest, approximately five hundred miles off the Alaskan coast.

While here at Kodiak awaiting takeoff, we are staying in an extremely large Quonset hut. The hut contains various sections such as a chapel area, a PX area, a dispensary, a kitchen with mess area, and a section for sleeping quarters for the personnel stationed here. There is also an entertainment area with a projector and a screen. Everything seems cozy within the hut, but it's a different world once one steps outside. This place is nothing like Anchorage. I'd hate to be stationed here. I'm sure there must be polar bears roaming around somewhere. They'd be hard to see in all this snow. We will be departing sometime tomorrow after breakfast.

September 15, 1950

It's now noon. We arrive at Tokyo, Japan today after leaving Kodiak yesterday. We will remain in Japan for two days prior to leaving for Korea. We have a chance to clean up, shave, shower and later see some of Tokyo. After I write to Cassie, I will go with a few others to take in some Tokyo sights. Sergeant Ford explained a few things to us. He was stationed here previously.

We found Tokyo to be a very large, very busy, and a very overpopulated city. Prior to returning to our quarters, we had a chance to buy some souvenirs. I'll ship them home tomorrow.

It is now 3:30 PM. We are leaving Tokyo by train and heading for Osaka, which is on the other end of the island. Osaka is a sea port where the troop ship that will take us to Korea is docked. Each day we are getting closer and closer.

Meanwhile, according to news reports, the First Marine Division has made a surprise invasion of Inchon, Korea, routing the North Korean forces guarding Inchon. Catching them by surprise was a big help. Meeting little resistance, the Marines are continuing their drive toward Seoul. They hope to link up with the army units around Seoul and assist them in defending it from advancing enemy forces.

The train ride lasted three and a half hours. We arrived at Osaka at 7:00 PM and will remain here overnight.

Korea: Frozen Hell on Earth

<u>September 17, 1950</u>

Having had our breakfast, we are departing Osaka in a small overcrowded ship. What a miserable ride this will be. In addition to being so crowded, this is by far not the cleanest ship in the world. The water between Japan and Korea is extremely rough. By the looks of things I'm sure that there will be some seasick soldiers. Many will be losing their breakfasts before long.

Sergeant Ford and I are still together, along with several others that were stationed in Fort Meade. None of us know into which unit we will be assigned. We will receive our assignment orders when we arrive at Pusan. Some will go to the Twenty-fourth Infantry Division, some to the Twenty-fifth. A few will go to the First Cavalry, and others will go to various support units.

Sergeant Ford and I are hoping to be assigned to the same unit. Many on board are also hoping to be assigned with friends they've made since leaving the States. The anchor is raised, and we are on our way.

Japan is beginning to fade out of sight. The water continues to be rough and choppy. People are beginning to lean over the railing getting sick. I'm afraid this includes me!

Bill Ford just gave me a peeled orange saying that it will settle my stomach. I'm not sure that it will, but the orange is sweet and juicy. Usually citrus fruits or anything sour helps seasickness, but not this time. I, along with others, suffered through it.

Now that the ship seems to have settled into a smoother ride, I have started to write a letter. I don't feel much like writing, but I'll take a crack at it. The letter will be mailed upon reaching Pusan. (See letter to Cassie dated September 18, 1950.)

<u>September 19, 1950 (Initial Enemy Fire)</u>

Thank God that boat ride is over. We docked at the harbor of Pusan today at 10:00 AM. We had eaten our breakfast earlier and now, while still on board, we are receiving our unit assignments. It seems as if our wishes came true. Both Sergeant Ford and I are going to Company G, Seventh Cavalry Regiment. We have been informed the Seventh Cavalry is on line, in action, defending Pusan. They are on line with the Twenty-fourth Infantry Division. We are to depart for the front as soon as the trucks arrive. The front, better known as the Pusan Perimeter, is approximately forty to sixty miles north from Pusan.

The trucks arrived at 12 noon. We will depart as soon as the loading is finished. We all are getting a little hungry, as we haven't eaten since early on the ship. They will initiate our arrival by providing our first meal in an open field. Our meal will be brought to us somewhere on the road.

As the convoy moves out we can see orchards of trees with large, beautiful red apples. We have learned that the apple trees are cultivated by farmers carrying "honey buckets." These buckets are filled with human waste gathered from outhouses and used for cultivation. The same method is used for growing rice. All of a sudden the apples do not look so tempting. But I am told that they are delicious.

Shortly after 1:00 PM the convoy stops and we are told to dismount. The kitchen truck has caught up with us. We gather our mess kits and line up for our hot meal. As we begin to eat we come under mortar fire, forcing us to disperse away from the trucks. The trucks seem to be drawing the fire, which lasts less than a minute. Luckily there are no casualties, but it does ruin everyone's meal.

I hated to lose my cup of hot chocolate. Thank God the rounds landed short. If the enemy had a higher O.P. (Observation Point), they would have had better results.

This is my first taste of enemy fire since fighting against the Germans in Yugoslavia in 1944.

September 20, 1950

Here we are at Taegu. We arrived here at 3:00 PM and

joined our unit. What a relief it is to get off the truck. The trip was very dusty and bumpy, and with exception of the mortar fire while we were eating, it was uneventful.

Sergeant Ford and I meet Captain J. Mulaison, commanding officer of Company G. Captain Mulaison, age thirty-two, is a six-foot, 180-pound, young officer with sandy blond hair who could make anyone's football team.

After a brief question and answer period regarding our prior service and additional background information, Sergeant Ford and I were introduced to our respective platoon leaders. Each of us is assigned as a platoon sergeant, replacing sergeants who were temporarily acting in this capacity. I am the sergeant of the Second Platoon and Sergeant Ford has the Third. We were then introduced to First Sergeant Robert Gray, a six-year army veteran.

It will take a while to meet and familiarize ourselves with the squad leaders and platoon members. All are spread out, right and left, and in position along the perimeter line. Most of the members are merely boys in their late teens or early twenties.

Both Sergeant Ford and I, as well as the first sergeant, being thirty years old, are the oldest members in the company. We learned that this is the situation in most of the companies within the regiment.

The First Cavalry Division, commanded by Brigadier General Hap Gay, is holding Taegu against a strong enemy force. There is firing taking place out in front, but I'm not sure where it's coming from. I am extremely nervous, this being my second day on line. But I notice that most everyone is nervous and on edge. I'm hoping that there are no itchy fingers among the men, which could shoot at imaginary targets and disclose our position. This is my first action under combat conditions since World War II. This is quite a different war; the conditions are quite different. If I said I wasn't nervous or scared, I'd be lying. Before we arrived, the company had a number of recent casualties, including one platoon sergeant KIA.

The weather is very hot and dusty. I haven't had a chance to wash after the dusty ride here yesterday. I sure could use a bath, and by the looks and appearances of the other men, everybody could. I knew Korea would be hell. The nearest water is the Naktong River, which is ten miles away. We will be moving out toward the river tomorrow morning.

September 23, 1950

We have been here in place for the past three days holding the ground along the Naktong River. We receive orders to cross the river and push on toward the enemy facing us. As we move out we were surprised at our successful drive, forcing the North Koreans to give ground. With our drive forward we link up with the forward elements of the U.S. Seventh Division. We continue to advance with only sporadic fire and little other resistance from the enemy.

Moving forward we see scattered dead and wounded enemies along the route. Some of the bodies are shot as we move on. That's because some North Koreans pretend to be dead or wounded, then shoot or throw grenades at those who pass by. Quite a few have been captured. They have been placed in holding areas until they are transported to POW compounds at Division Headquarters.

The hot weather is causing the dead Chinese to smell bad, almost nauseating. In addition to the stench, there are enormous black flies buzzing around the corpses. I've never seen such large flies before. Very irritating. Thankfully, we keep moving forward.

The weather is still extremely warm if not hot, with a lot of choking dust. Rain would hold the dust down, but rain, I am told, makes everything muddy, sloppy, and slippery and makes it difficult for vehicles to function. This, among other things, I will learn as time goes by.

September 26 - 28, 1950

We have managed to beat back the enemy considerably. Taegu is safe for the time being. The Second Battalion is leaving its Taegu position to join the main body of the First Cavalry Division at Seoul. Bitter street and house to house fighting is taking place when we arrive. The First Marine Division has joined in the fight. The crack of rifle fire and bursts of machine gun fire are coming from all directions. People are being hit and falling here and there. There are many casualties on both sides.

It seems like a nightmare. There is total confusion. Cries for medics can be heard coming from all directions. The medics have their hands full. Several of them are wounded.

Finally, after two days and countless casualties, Seoul is again retaken. Quite a number of civilians have been tortured, the bodies mutilated by the enemy before they retreat.

October 2 - 12, 1950

After considerable action around Seoul, mostly mop up, the Second Battalion is placed in reserve. We need rest and replacements. Finally a chance to clean up, shave, rest, and write some letters. Turns are taken, a few at a time, to go to the river for baths. Finally, it's my turn. I can hardly wait. The water is cold, but the bath is necessary.

The weather is beginning to change. The nights are especially cold and damp. It's really rough getting up in the morning. The smell of hot coffee brewing helps to wake a person up. The coffee hits the spot, but it's nothing like being back in garrison.

What I wouldn't give for a ham and egg breakfast with coffee and toast. But that's dreaming! One does a lot of dreaming here in this hell hole. I'm forever dreaming of Cassie and of home.

We just had mail call. I received a package of pepperoni and a pair of fur lined gloves from Cassie. I had requested these earlier in my letters to her. With the weather getting colder, the gloves will come in handy. My pepperoni doesn't last too long. It seems as if everyone knows I received it. Oh well, it was good while it lasted.

Now it's time to clean weapons. Time to check and oil all moving parts and make a list of the shortages. I remind the squad leaders to make sure the each man has an extra pair of socks on his person when we move out, and tell them to pull an inspection of each man's weapon, making sure they are clean and in good working order. The rain, mud, and dust are doing a number on the weapons. We are forever cleaning them.

October 13 - 16, 1950
Moving north from Seoul we cross the Thirty-eighth parallel, being the first American unit to do so. There is a rumor that some units have detected Chinese.

Up to this point we were not aware of, nor have we seen, any Chinese involved. Among other forces in Korea are some token units from United Nations countries furnishing personnel for the United Nations Command. Among these are soldiers from Greece, Turkey, and Australia. Earlier today a company size Turkish unit passed by our area heading north. We were alerted that they would be coming so that we didn't fire on them.

The immediate terrain north of the Thirty-eighth parallel is no different from the terrain to the south. We see one hill after another and one mountain following another. All are steep, barren, and extremely rocky.

We are moving north toward Kaesong to join the main body of the Seventh Cavalry Regiment. They are deployed in a perimeter guarding the approaches of Kaesong. This is in territory controlled by the Chinese, detected by our G-2.

Company G is moving, single file, along the winding road and along the base of the high ground. We are suddenly pinned down by machine gun fire from the high

House to house fighting in retaking Seoul,
September 26-28, 1950.

September 1950, walking toward the
Naktong River for a much needed bath.

September 1950. Shortly after my arrival at Company G, Seventh Cavalry, along the Pusan Perimeter

October 14, 1950. Taken the day after the First Cavalry Division crossed the Thirty-eighth parallel.

ground at the right. We all hit the ground, but are unable to move, for there is no cover. The bullets keep hitting all around. The ground, being hard, rock solid, and frozen, makes digging in useless. The commanding officer and the platoon leader are up ahead of the winding column. No one has been hit yet, though the bullets are bouncing all around, hitting the ground in front of us.

A couple of mortar rounds fly over our heads, exploding on the hill behind us. I can't lay here praying not to get hit. Corporal Riggs, a young squad leader, is close to me. I tell him to follow me with his squad, plus the second squad. We run, zigzagging across the open field, toward the base of the high ground.

Reaching the base we fan out, dispersing, a squad on each side, closing in toward the firing. We locate and surprise two gun emplacements manned by several North Koreans whom we were able to rout, killing two of them. During this encounter, none of my men are hurt.

Returning to our respective places in the column, I inform Captain Mulaison of the action taken. After taking note, the company continues on toward Kaesong to fulfill our mission.

[For this action I was awarded the Bronze Star Medal with Oak Leaf Cluster. See Appendix 1.]

October 17 - 19, 1950

The weather is continually getting much colder and more miserable. The sleet and freezing rain are making it more difficult not only for the vehicles, but for the men. Thank God for the ponchos. In my opinion, next to the rifle the poncho is a solder's best friend. They not only help to keep you dry, but are good windbreakers, in addition to being used as overhead covers in foxholes and as sleeping mats. These benefits are only realized in weather like this. The temperature today is unusually cold for the month of October.

The Eighth Army, under General Walker, is ordered to

move toward Pyongyang, the capitol of North Korea. The First Cavalry has been made a part of the Eighth Army. Moving north, we are losing men due to frostbitten fingers and toes. The weather seems to be affecting the enemy as well. At one point approximately 100 Chinese soldiers surrendered to us in a group. They were hungry, cold, without ammunition, and almost frozen. Captain Mulaison delegated me with six members to guard these prisoners until relieved by Division Military Police. Fortunately, the rain has stopped, and the temperature is slightly warmer.

Guarding these prisoners for two days was quite an experience. Being hungry and cold, they became quite restless, and we were in enemy territory. I was concerned that the prisoners would bolt at any time. Luckily, they didn't. Meanwhile, my company, along with the Eighth Army, kept moving farther and farther away, on the way to Pyongyang.

What a relief! Division Headquarters finally arrived and the prisoners were turned over. We were given a supply of K-rations, as we had used up our supply during the two days. Now to find our way to the Seventh Cavalry, wherever they may be. They should be near Pyongyang, northwest from our present position. We can't stay with Division Headquarters as they are not moving from here until ordered by Command Headquarters. Our best way to reach our unit is to hitchhike, catching rides with American or UN vehicles heading north. To do this we have to split up. Most of the vehicles are overloaded jeeps with room for one or two passengers only.

I was fortunate to catch a ride on a Twenty-fourth Infantry jeep taking communication supplies to a battalion in reserve near Kaesong. Here I was able to spend the night. The following morning I got a ride on a two-and-a half-ton truck with supplies going to First Cavalry Division Headquarters at Suriwon. The Seventh Cavalry Regiment is ten miles north in a battle for Pyongyang.

Shooting can be heard. Overhead are planes, providing air strikes. From the division hospital I catch a ride in an ambulance going to the Seventh Cavalry Regiment.

After two days of hitching rides and existing on K-rations, I finally catch up with the Second Battalion. Two of the men who were with me arrived earlier, the other four are listed as missing, at least temporarily. Company G is deployed along the high ground at the outskirts of Pyongyang. Pyongyang had been liberated while we were with the prisoners. I have rejoined my platoon, which had been taken over by Sergeant William Link during my absence. For now all is quiet. During the lull I take head count and find that there are two missing as a result of the latest action. Hopefully they are only missing, not dead, or laying somewhere wounded. I will need to check with the Battalion Aid Station for a recent record of wounded. Sergeant Ford also has two men missing.

October 23, 1950

There has been no action in this area for the past two days or any record of the missing men. We must continue to carry them as missing or captured.

We are ordered to hold in place until further notice. That order is not hard to take. It's a relief to be able to relax (?) for a while. If it wasn't for the cold, I could almost enjoy it. I received several letters from Cassie and family. One letter contained a clipping from the *Baltimore Sun* stating that many people consider the Korean conflict merely a "police action" rather than a war. (They should make that comment to the parents or wives whose sons or husbands were killed in action.)

October 26, 1950

We have been ordered to break camp. Our battalion is to move on toward Chinnan-Po, north of Pyongyang. This is the heart of enemy territory. The few days of rest spoiled us, but it did refresh us for our mission.

The weather is bitter cold and many of our vehicles are stalled or bogged down in snow or ruts. We are meeting stiff enemy resistance as we move forward. Many wounded are passing us, being carried to the rear for evacuation. It's very depressing to see the dead and wounded Americans.

Earlier I gave our mail clerk two letters to be mailed. He never got the chance. He was shot through the eye and killed before leaving the area. The letters were retrieved by the medics and taken to battalion for mailing. Many men envied the mail clerk's job!

October 29, 1950

We arrive at Chinnan-Po and immediately dig in, not knowing what to expect. What a chore this is, digging in into this frozen ground.

I'm surprised how well the young soldiers follow instructions, obey orders, and at their overall performances. Many act like seasoned veterans. A person learns quickly here how to survive and preserve!

I am scheduled to take out a twelve-man reconnaissance patrol. We are to ride in a truck to a spot four or five miles ahead of the company's perimeter, there to dismount and scout the area, checking for any visible traps, snipers, or enemy build up, and return with any information found.

At approximately 3:00 PM, after briefing my men and a final equipment check, I am informed that Sergeant Davis would lead the patrol in my place. The patrol leaves at 3:30 PM. This give me a chance to write to Cassie.

The weather is wet and miserable. It has been raining for some time, causing all roads to be slippery. The recon patrol, returning from its mission, ran into a muddy-terrain problem. The truck, attempting to negotiate a sharp turn, overturned, injuring many, including Sgt. Davis. The injured, four from my platoon, were sent back to the regimental aid station for treatment and evaluation.

Casualties from the latest action, the present injuries, and the loss of personnel from frost bite, have taken their toll. We need replacements!

The company commander informs us at a critique that forward elements of the Twenty-fourth Division have advanced within a few miles of the Yalu River. This is the border line between North Korea and China. It is also a Chinese/North Korean stronghold.

Meanwhile, the second platoon received a new platoon leader. He is Lt. S. Jackson, a pudgy, thirty-year-old army veteran from Pittsburgh, Pennsylvania. We nicknamed him Stonewall Jackson. I'm sure that after two or three weeks he will not be so pudgy. No one is fat in Second Platoon—especially not after climbing up and down these God-forsaken mountains.

The CO also informs us that we have to move out towards Anju at 5:00 AM. Anju is the heart of enemy territory. Needless to say, the men are not exactly anxious to get there! Neither am I! I realize that any encounter could by my last.

October 30, 1950

Our battalion has reached the main body (First and Third Battalions) of the Seventh Cavalry Regiment. They are already in a bloody battle with the enemy around Anju. Things are really hot and hectic. Fire is coming from all directions. From behind the crest of hills to our front, black smoke can be seen rising up from our artillery fire. Reaching the top of the crest, my platoon is deployed, facing the high ground in front and firing into anything that resembles a person's form. They fire on anything moving.

It is bitter cold, but the battle for survival helps to minimize the weather, though it is an enemy also. We are receiving some casualties, particularly from enemy mortar fire. I'm certain that the Chinese are losing much more due to our superior fire power and artillery strikes. I'm not sure if that is any consolation. Our medics have their hands full! What a nightmare this is! Not just a nightmare, but plain hell!

We gradually move forward, causing the Chinese to give ground, thanks to the desperately needed air support bombing their positions. Moving forward, we detect human bodies scattered everywhere along the surrounding frozen ground. Most have been hit by air strikes, artillery, and/or our own mortars. This weather is affecting the enemy as well as us. There are wounded and frozen bodies along the way. The cold weather minimizes the sickening smell of human blood!

We continue moving north towards the Yalu River, to relieve the surrounded elements of Gen. John Church's Twenty-fourth Division. The temperature is near zero. The bitter, biting wind is torture. There is no shelter from it. It's so difficult to keep in any order or in contact. This is really hell, frozen hell!

My feet and my fingers are numb from the cold. However, I am not alone in this. Most of the men, if not all, seem to be grumbling, shivering, and searching for any spot sheltered from the wind as we bed down for the night.

October 31 - November 2, 1950

After a miserable, cold night we move out. Marching most of the morning, we finally reach Unsan, just north of the Chongchon River. Approximately forty miles north is the Yalu River. So far we are receiving only sporadic resistance. Something is not right. Heavy resistance was anticipated. According to G-2 reports, this is prime enemy territory. All indications predicted that a fierce fight would take place.

Lieutenant Jackson and I have just returned from company CP (Command Post), receiving a critique and final instructions from Captain Mulaison. We were told that President Truman ordered General MacArthur not to attempt to cross Yalu River into China, at least not with

American troops, though there is evidence that Chinese volunteers are working with and aiding the North Korean army. The Chinese soldiers appear to be much better and more disciplined than the North Koreans.

It appears as though the G-2 information regarding the enemy strength was correct. Early morning, November 1, we were surprised by a major counter attack by strong Chinese forces. We were outnumbered many times over. All hell broke loose. We were forced to withdraw as were other units on line with us. We recrossed Chongchon River, which we had only recently taken. It's so difficult to maneuver in this frigid weather and icy terrain.

Keeping track of personnel is almost impossible. The Chinese keep advancing in great numbers. Our artillery and mortar fire are preventing us from being overrun, though we are receiving casualties. Thanks to the steady bombardment, the Chinese to our front are temporarily halted. Other units are not so lucky. The bombing gives us a chance to pull back.

Moving back a few miles, we encamp in a logical area, dig in the best we can, and position ourselves. It's so good to halt even for a little while. Not only is my platoon tired, but everyone is physically exhausted from being constantly on the go. In this area, not too far from the enemy, we take the chance to regroup and assess our losses. I'm not certain how many men are lost from Company G. The company is scattered, with stragglers coming in. I am missing two men from my platoon. The difficult thing is not knowing whether they were killed or only missing. I hate to think of them being captured during our retreat. I'm told that the platoon medic has been hit. That's bad news. I don't know how soon we'll get a replacement, but is imperative that one comes.

We have just received word that the Third Battalion of the Eighth Cavalry, which was to our front, is overrun by the Chinese. They are involved in hand-to-hand combat.

Their commanding officer, Maj. J. Ormond, was wounded severely. I hate to imagine what the outcome will be. This is a terrible fate.

November 23, 1950

We move back farther to another clearing. Things are quiet in our sector, but we hear firing nearby. Today is Thanksgiving Day and miracles do happen! Our Thanksgiving dinner is brought to us in the field. Turkey with all the dressing and other things to go with it. What a treat! This is the first hot meal we've had for some time. The cold weather is cooling our dinner rapidly, but it still is better than the constant K- and C-rations. Even in the cold we are enjoying our dinner. It's difficult to imagine that the enemy is just over the hill, where bitter fighting is taking place. While eating, we have to keep dispersed from each other. This is to minimize casualties should a surprise mortar attack occur. Fortunately, there is no attack.

November 26, 1950

From almost out of nowhere the Chinese attack again with superior numbers. Many casualties are inflicted on the Eighth Army units. Particularly hard hit is the Twenty-fourth Division. They are on line with us and the ROK Army. Mortar rounds are dropping near our area. We have to fall back a little farther. Thank God the mortars stop. There are no casualties at this encounter, but the freezing weather and the cold wind are almost unbearable!

Being outnumbered, we reluctantly had to give ground and withdraw even farther. Our main concern is not to be cut off or overrun. Maintaining any unity is nearly impossible. There is no let up from the bitter wind. Staying close to each other is comforting, but not good strategy. Enemy mortars are hitting here and there; however, there are no casualties in the Second Platoon as of yet today.

The word just received is that our line of defense is considerably weaker. The Fifth Cavalry Regiment, which was sent to rescue the overrun Third Battalion, Eighth Cavalry, was badly roughed up in the effort. It had to be withdrawn from the combat sector until resupplied and reorganized. Many men were lost. We learned that Maj. Ormond has died from his wounds. What a tragedy! I don't know when this war will end or what the outcome will be. I hope and pray that he did not die in vain!

November 27, 1950

It is officially established that China has entered the war. Thousands of Chinese Communist Forces (CCF) have crossed the Yalu River from China, attacking all of the UN forces with full force. We are outnumbered many times over and are forced to retreat, falling back constantly. In our effort to get away from the immediate area as quickly as possible (some call it bugging out), personnel are climbing on any vehicle heading south. All vehicles have turned out to be "personnel carriers," be they jeeps, trucks, or, especially, tanks. All are overloaded, making them difficult to steer and difficult for the drivers to negotiate sharp curves. The bitter cold, icy roads, deep snow, and slippery terrain are playing havoc with the vehicles. Many are bogged down in snow, in ruts, and in ditches. Some have to be abandoned. Others have overturned causing even more injuries to personnel. We can hear cries for help from those hurt. There is total chaos and confusion. Many of the men are in a state of shock.

This condition does not lessen until the next day, when we are far enough away to regroup, reorganize, and attempt to locate any stragglers. Lt. Jackson asks for a head count. I can only give him an estimate. [Some of the missing will never be accounted for.]

Many men, including a few in my platoon, are suffering from the cold and exposure, which are adding to the difficulties of reorganizing. It is difficult to recognize some of the men, especially those with beards, which are now covered by small balls of ice, much of it due to the exhaling of the breath which freezes. While being forced back our artillery is pounding enemy lines and positions, impeding their advance.

A few miles down the road, reaching some high ground, we stop, assemble, and regroup to assess our losses as accurately as possible. We take positions along the ridge. What the units to our right and left are doing is unknown at this time. The rugged terrain is making it difficult for us to communicate with each other. There is no sign of the enemy to our front, thus giving us more time to organize. Those who are unable to function due to wounds, frost bite, exhaustion, or whatever, are moved to a safe area until the arrival of trucks for their evacuation to Regimental Aid Stations for evaluation and care.

Meanwhile, the Second Battalion has been pulled back to our present location. We secure our position as best as possible while reorganizing. Our position is not too secure, having no contact with units at our left or right flanks. The Chinese could easily encircle us if they knew our circumstances or predicament. Some units have been overrun, I'm sure. We are to remain at this location until ordered otherwise by Command Headquarters.

I have received some good news. I've been informed that Specialist J. Howard, a medic, will be joining our platoon. Medics are a necessity. A good medic is as good as an angel!

November 28 - 29, 1950

We received orders to move out toward Sunchon to aid the Second Division. They are in close combat with the Chinese and, being outnumbered, are facing disaster. They really need reinforcements. The Seventh Cavalry, led by Colonel Bill Harris, is being dispatched to help relieve this situation.

Our advance towards Sunchon is greatly slowed down by the large number of refugees clogging the roads. Mixed among the refugees are soldiers of the ROK army, bugging out, heading south away from battle. We have learned that their unit was attacked and shattered by the Chinese around the Anju area. It appears as if they have either lost or thrown away their weapons. The Chinese kill anyone found with a weapon if he is not a North Korean soldier. I was informed of this by the leader of the ROK platoon assigned to us.

The Second Battalion arrives at Singchang, near Sunchon. We are immediately swarmed by a hoard of Chinese, attacking from the hills. We are forced back, receiving casualties, several close to me. We some how manage to pull back to the high ground to our rear, dragging and assisting our wounded. A Chinese full scale attack is anticipated at any minute. All we can do is wait.

The Third Battalion of the Seventh Cavalry, led by Col. Jim Lynch, came to our rescue. They came with tanks and AA vehicles, blasting the Chinese, halting them in place. The field is covered with an unknown amount of dead enemy bodies. The Third Battalion was to our rear, in reserve, in the event they were needed. They were needed, and how! The phrase "the cavalry to the rescue" was never more evident!

We learned that this action spared the fate of the Second Division, preventing a tragic disaster. The Chinese pulled most of their troops away from the Second Division in order to face the Seventh Cavalry. This enabled the Second Division's survivors to complete their withdrawal through Sunchon.

Though the Chinese have been temporarily halted, we are not out of the woods yet. We are outnumbered, deep in enemy territory. It is beginning to snow heavily and it's freezing cold. If this isn't hell, I don't know what is. It's below zero and so cold it's even hard to think straight. But our main concern now is that the Chinese don't overrun this hill.

As difficult as it is to dig foxholes in the snow, all platoons must take defensive positions, encircling the hill.

Capt. Mulaison's orders are to hold the hill at all costs. No pulling back unless ordered by battalion headquarters or overrun by the Chinese. The men grumble about digging, knowing that we may be pulling out at any moment. I can't blame them for they are tired and cold, but it's for their own safety. I pair off with Sgt. Link and we begin digging.

November 31 - December 21, 1950

Between November and December we are in constant battle with the Chinese. We are also fighting the weather. Our battles are more of the defensive type, as we are being pushed back gradually. The retreat is being labeled a "strategic withdrawal," as our mortars and artillery fire, while pulling back, are costing the Chinese dearly. The air strikes are particularly doing a fine job and have caused the Chinese to cease their advance. However, due to our retreat, Pyongyang had to be surrendered. We had just liberated it a month earlier. What a waste of time and personnel!

December 22 - 26, 1950

The events that occurred the past few days are very discouraging. Not only have we lost Pyongyang, but I have been informed that Gen. Walton "Bulldog" Walker has been killed. He was the Eighth Army commander, killed in a jeep accident while checking front line conditions. This is a big loss. Gen. Walker was well liked by everyone. He had a very distinguished and brilliant military career.

Today, December 24, is Christmas Eve and bitter cold. We are deployed around the high ground we are holding, anticipating an enemy attack at any moment. However, all is still and quiet, almost eerie. Our recon patrol, sent out earlier, should be returning soon. I have just finished a letter to Cassie, and not having a Christmas card, I sketched a Christmas scene, wishing her a happy holiday. I don't know when or if the letter will go out. This waiting, the quiet, stillness, and the cold are nerve-racking. I don't understand why there is no sign of the enemy. Perhaps the Chinese are honoring our holiday! Wishful thinking. The recon patrol has returned with no encounters or any sign of the enemy.

We were informed today, December 26th, that the new Eighth Army commander is to be Gen. Matthew Ridgway, another great officer of World War II fame. Men who know him say that he is very gung-ho. He was given a nickname of Hand Grenade Matt. He always has a hand grenade hanging from his shoulder strap as part of his uniform.

The Chinese have discontinued their offense for the time being. It's been quiet for the past two days. No Chinese or North Korean troops have been observed; however, we are constantly on alert. We have learned one important element regarding Chinese strategy. They do not maneuver or travel much during daylight. They stay put, undercover, traveling at night or early dawn. They usually sneak up, surprising the enemy with yelling, banging, whistles, and horns blowing. If it wasn't for their small arms and hand grenades killing and wounding, one would think they were celebrating their new year.

However, for now everything is quiet. Our cooks have managed to bring us a hot breakfast. What a treat! They have also brought radios. With our breakfast and coffee they played music for us.

We heard for the first time "The Tennessee Waltz" sung by the new singing rage, Miss Patti Page. What a nice way to start a morning. Cold or no cold, Patti is everybody's sweetheart! What a morale booster!

January 3, 1951
The Second Platoon is dug in around the high ground two miles in front of the battalion. We have been here two days, expecting an unknown number of advancing Chinese. Instructions are to pull back, using the designated route once contact is made. Ahead each side of the designated route is mined and barbed wired. All is

the hills around me. I have my men all dug in in their fox holes. We have been here 2 days and nights now. The Chinese are on their way. We are the out post line - that is - we are about 2 miles in front of our regiment. I have 5-0 men with me. The enemy will hit us first - or else we will fire on them as soon as we see them - then pull back to our regiment. I hope every thing works out all right. It will if they don't cut us off (If you get this letter - then you will know that we made it O.K.)

at night for we have only one trail to use to get back to our lines. Every thing else is mined and barbed wired. But we will make quiet until contact is finally made. We pull back to the battalion perimeter using the route. The Chinese are up to something big, this being their forward element.

January 4, 1951

The quiet did not last too long. It seems as though the Chinese managed to regroup and resupply their losses during the lull. They have managed to start our new year off with a bang.

Today, with new troops, the Chinese have launched a major offensive. At least we are told that it is major, forcing us back even farther. It isn't just the Second Battalion being hit. Our commanding officer informs that all the units on line are facing a similar fate, having to retreat. This means that the Chinese are attacking on a broad line. If they manage to break through we face encirclement. We are forced back still farther. To prevent an encirclement we continue moving back.

This retreat has forced us to go south of Seoul, which we have to give up. Our units are really chopped up, sustaining huge losses. Especially hard hit is the Nineteenth Infantry Regiment at our right flank. Several men who were with me in the Third Cavalry at Fort Meade were assigned to the Nineteenth. These include Lt. Paar and Pfc.'s Marales and Spivey. I pray that they made it through okay. All are good men and fine soldiers.

We are giving up much of the territory taken earlier. This yo-yo type warfare is very discouraging and frustrating. It sure is lowering troop morale. With our capability, our aircraft, and our armament, we should not be fighting a limited war. If allowed to go all out, we could win it.

January 7, 1951

Today is my first wedding anniversary. What a place to be on an anniversary. We are still in retreat. Many of our units are surrounded. But help has arrived. We are now receiving the air support that was desperately needed. The air strikes are having a great effect on Chinese maneuverability. Occasionally, some of the strikes land close to and on our lines and positions. It's difficult for the air crew to know where our lines end and the enemy's begin. We must, therefore, disclose our positions with large orange markers. I'm sure that the enemy's O.P.s appreciate this, but we can't have our cake and eat it, too.

Some areas, due to rocky terrain and steep hillsides, are difficult targets. The strikes are not too effective. However, the napalm bombs on these areas are very effective. They rouse the Chinese out of their cover and various hiding places, making them easy targets. The air strikes have temporarily halted the Chinese attack, at least in our area. Things seem to be happening elsewhere, but I can't tell what or against whom or what unit. Firing by heavy guns can be heard. As darkness approaches, temperatures drop even more. Soon dark clouds are beginning to form. It seems as though we will get some rain before morning.

Upon waking up, we find it is very cold, with a drizzly rain. The rain soon turns into freezing rain. It's very slippery and difficult to walk.

This war and climate are nothing like those of Europe. Some of the disadvantages in Korea are the inhospitable weather conditions, both in winter and summer. Winters are extremely cold and windy. Summers, during rainy seasons, are hot and steamy or exceptionally dry and dusty. Then there are the rice paddies everywhere that must be waded through time and again. The paddies stink of human feces used as fertilizer. Last, but not least, are the civilians who wage warfare against the Americans. North Korean soldiers, intermingling with civilian refugees are difficult to detect until they throw a grenade. By then, it's too late!

January 8 - 25, 1951

American casualties receiving first aid by
medics and chaplain at front line aid station.

my last letter to you,
and every bit of it has been awful
On the 24th. of Jan. our division
made a counter attack on the Chinese
and since then Darling – we have
been pushing forward. We retook
40 miles that the Chinese had
taken from us earlier. The past
4 days we have had some of the blood-
iest fighting since before Thanksgiving.
You should see the Chinese we have

killed. They #2 are all over the fields
and hills However we have lost
some men too But no where near
as much as the enemy.

After considerable action back and forth we stop and encamp. We need to regroup and reorganize and fill our vacancies with the replacement personnel that have arrived. We are still receiving very young soldiers, with two or three veterans occasionally.

On January 15, the First Cavalry initiates a counterattack. We are successful in driving the Chinese back, gaining ground. On January 23 the Eighth Army, together with the ROK Army, launch a major attack. This drive, known as Operation Thunderbolt, drives the Chinese back toward the Han River. Many, many Chinese are killed, as are Americans.

During this push my platoon leader, Lieutenant "Stonewall" Jackson was killed. We lost a fine officer and a major loss to Company G. Lieutenant Jackson is my second platoon leader killed in the past three months.

What a terrible loss. Such a good combat officer, well liked and respected by everyone. He appears so forlorn lying there, his uniform too large for his body. He lost over thirty pounds in just over two months. Never got the time to get the proper size. Our new platoon leader will be Lt. Grey.

February 2, 1951

This is the sixth day of our counter attack. In pushing the Chinese back we have recaptured much of the ground lost earlier. Many Chinese have been killed during this drive, but we have our share of casualties, also. Another big blow to Company G! First Sergeant Gray is reported to have been killed by mortar fire. I feel bad. He was a good friend and a good soldier. He will be missed as will the others that have been reported killed. I firmly believe that Korea is as close to hell as anyone can get!

Our advance forward is impeded and slowed down considerably. Countless refugees going the opposite way, clog the small or only roads by hauling their possessions in carts and wagons, some being lucky enough to still possess a few livestock or other animals. Most carry their belongings on their backs using A frames.

I feel sorry for these people, especially for the very young and very old. They are innocent people, victims of a terrible war, being constantly uprooted and displaced with all their belongings gone. Most are grieving for lost family members, many of whom they witnessed being murdered and mutilated by their own people.

February 7, 1951

Our offense, which has been going so well, comes to a stand still when we reach Inchon. We are confronted by a dug-in enemy on Hill 381 and are forced to dig in place. At the commanding officer's briefing we are informed that the enemy is strong in this area and has just recently taken this hill from the Greek battalion after a bloody battle.

Our mission is to attack Hill 381 and dislodge the Chinese, for we need access to the road. Following some tremendous tank, artillery, and heavy mortar bombardment, the Second Battalion, moving up from each side of the hill, was able to dislodge the enemy after a close range fire fight. Taking this hill, Company G had three men killed and twenty-two wounded. We are losing men before we even get to know them well. However, there were no losses from the Second Platoon today. (See my letter to Cassie dated February 7, 1951).

Moving on, we see dead Chinese scattered along the way. Checking a few that are close by, we notice that they have American uniforms under their quilted ones. These were most likely removed from dead-American soldiers or American prisoners. It's very, very cold. Our breath is like cigarette smoke being exhaled from our mouths. Smoking is very difficult, as the cigarettes tend to stick to lips. It is also dangerous in that it tends to draw enemy fire.

Farther along we spot three Chinese who had cut down pine trees and tied them around their waists as

are there some where. We chased
them out of these hills. Night before
last we took two hills from them. I
told you in my last letter that we were
going on another attack. Well, we took
those two hills and we had a hard
time doing it. It cost us 3 men
killed and 22 wounded. You aught
to see the dead Chinese on top of the
hill. We had to spend the night
right there on the hill and the dead
Chinese were all around us. Honey,
it was horrible. Underneath their
Chinese uniforms they had American
clothes. I suppose they got them from
American prisoners

October 1950, Chinnan-Po. I'm center, rear, Sgts. Bill Ford and Snuffy Gray kneeling.

October 1950, near Pyongyang. Prisoners captured in bitter cold, the one with guitar was one of three camouflaged by pine trees tied around their waists. This was a photo among his possessions.

Korea: Frozen Hell on Earth

camouflage. We take them as prisoners. They are almost frozen. They are surprised that we don't kill them after capture, having been told by their officers not to give up, for the Americans would kill them. This is interpreted to us by an ROK soldier, the leader of the ROK platoon attached to our company. He spoke and understood Chinese, as well as a little English.

<u>February 13, 1951</u>

Moving up along the road, we reach Yoju, near the Han River. Here Company G is involved in several fire fights. In capturing a nearby high ground we have more members wounded. These are carried to the foot of the hill (Hill 381) for immediate first aid and evacuation. Just more shortages that have to be filled. We can never remain at full strength, losing eleven men during this encounter. I came near to being wounded when a bullet grazed my elbow, tearing through my jacket! Close call! (See letter to Cassie, received February 27, 1951.)

The battalion's next objective given to Col. Calloway is Hill 578, which is about six miles ahead. Hill 578 is a Chinese stronghold having command of the rugged surrounding terrain and overlooking Mugam. It has to be taken. Heavy bombardment and artillery barrage had failed to dislodge the dug in Chinese. An infantry type of attack is needed to root out the defenders. This objective is for us tomorrow morning. Most of the men are extremely exhausted at this point. A few hours of sleep is needed. Rested or not, we move out early tomorrow.

<u>February 14, 1951</u>

Today is my thirty-first birthday. What a place to celebrate a birthday! What I wouldn't give to be home today. But we have a mission to perform. It's 5:00 AM. I am awakened by Lt. Grey to a very cold and miserable morning. My poncho and anything else exposed are covered with frozen dew. I awaken the rest of the platoon,

I didn't want to tell you this - but you asked me to let you know everything that happens here. Five days ago about 4:00 in the morning we attacked a hill that the Chinese were holding (381) We didn't think that they were quite as strong there as they were and we had to have the hill. It was still dark when we started up. We hoped to catch them sleeping. But instead; they set a trap for us. They saw us coming and waited till we got almost on them when they opened fire on us. The only thing that saved us from being wiped out was the darkness we lost 11 men. And I almost got hit in the arm   A bullet went past my elbow and through my jacket. How informing them that we are moving out shortly. After a breakfast of K-rations, we hit the road at 6:00 AM. Reaching the foot of Hill 578 at approximately 8:00 AM., we begin our assault. Col. Calloway estimates that the hill will be in our hands by early afternoon. How wrong his estimate proves to be! Resistance is met almost immediately. Going up hill against a dug-in enemy is slow and difficult. The best way to advance is by leapfrog method, one platoon at a time. The Chinese are shooting down, causing casualties. We return fire, deploying as we move forward. It's so difficult firing weapons while moving uphill, especially so on an unseen, well-camouflaged, and dug-in enemy. But we have to keep moving forward and uphill no matter what.

No sooner has the Second Platoon bypassed the First Platoon and deployed, when tragedy strikes. It still haunts me to this day. Sgt. Ford, my best friend and companion, is killed before my eyes, moments after passing me with the Third Platoon. He is approximately thirty feet from me. Initially, I thought that he only slipped on the frozen turf, falling backwards. Reaching him, I notice a neat hole in his forehead and bleeding from the back of his head. He is dead. I feel awful, sick in the stomach, and so helpless, but have to keep moving on. Others bodies are falling down. My platoon is spread out, and I don't see my platoon leader. Progress is very slow, limited to a creep and crawl. It's difficult to keep in contact with my men. I keep moving upward, looking for cover along the way. Sporadic fire keeps coming from the top. There is the occasional popping of a hand grenade. Some are landing too close for comfort. Fortunately, the grenades are the potato masher type, not like our grenades.

The day is fast passing by. It is now late afternoon, getting colder and darker. I can't see any form or outline of any platoon members or of Lt. Grey. He is probably ahead somewhere. Having no food since breakfast, I feel hungry. In my pocket is a K-ration chocolate bar. I dig it out and munch on it.

It's bitter cold and now close to 10:00 PM. It's very dark and I don't know how far I am from the top. There is an occasional flash of fire from there and return fire from another part of the hill. My feet feel as if they are freezing, almost numb. So are my fingers, which I rub constantly. Reaching a clump of bushes, I sit down. No matter what happens, I've got to remove my boots and rub my feet for circulation. They may already be frostbitten. Rubbing and rubbing soon brings circulation and feeling. Replacing my boots, I just sit and wait, beginning to get drowsy in spite of the cold. I must not give in to sleep, nor must I go down hill.

I move from one spot to another. I know I can't go forward all alone, believing I'm close to the top. This is the longest, loneliest, and darkest night of my life. I'll never forget my thirty-first birthday. I don't even know if I'll have another one. I keep praying that a hand grenade doesn't land close to me and that the Chinese don't come charging down. Due to the darkness, I don't believe that they have spotted me. Remaining still, my thoughts are of Cassie. Thinking of her gives me the strength to carry on. I keep praying that this nightmare will end and that I will survive.

Soon the moon breaks out from some parting clouds. To my right I observe a form approaching me. I can't recognize who it could be. I'm certain that it's not a Chinese or a North Korean because of the outline of the helmet. I have my rifle aimed at the form.

Soon he is close enough to be recognized. To my relief and surprise, it is Col. Calloway, the Battalion Commander. He is also surprised to see me. I am amazed to see our battalion commander here at the front lines. Col. Calloway has really earned my respect and has given me the confidence to carry on. He asks how many men are with me. I answer that I have no idea, having lost contact and control some time ago. He informs me that Lt. Grey is wounded and is at the bottom of the hill, as is

Approaching Hill 578 prior to assault, February 13, 1951.

Company G, Second Battalion, Seventh
Cavalry, taking Hill 578 on February 14, 1951.

Captain Mulaison, who is very ill. The colonel moves away, going downhill, saying that he has radioed for help and that this hill has to be taken. He also says that he passed some Company G men earlier around the bend. Perhaps that's where the return fire was coming from, but now I don't hear a thing. They could possibly be in a situation similar to mine. I haven't heard any rifle fire for some time except for the constant popping of grenades being launched by the Chinese. Occasionally there is a burst of machine-gun fire from the top. I hear when the grenades hit and bounce, exploding farther downhill. I can hardly wait, and I pray for daylight, to see the situation and rejoin my men.

Finally daybreak. I hear machine-gun and rifle fire coming from the saddle ridge between Hill 578 and the hill to the right. Tracer bullets are hitting the top of the hill. This firing must be the help Col. Calloway requested. I can make out the friendly uniforms. This really rejuvenates me. I see that I am less than a hundred yards from the top. I move forward, firing my rifle, as I go uphill. Upon reaching the top, I learn that the help is from Company K, Third Battalion. I recognize some of the men. Many enemy bodies are spread out over the mountain. Others have fled or vanished after being routed. It is now 6:00 AM.

Hill 578, the enemy stronghold, is in our hands, twenty-four hours after the assault began. Thank God I've survived another encounter!

There are only thirteen men of Company G at the top of the hill with me. Many were wounded, several were killed in action, with many others missing or disabled. Hill 578 and the bitter cold have taken their toll! For some reason, I can't stop shaking.

Right now I could go for some hot, black coffee. The kitchen truck, bringing breakfast, arrives when I reach the bottom of the hill. This nightmare has ended, at least for now. I thank God for again seeing me through, along with the others who survived.

February 15, 1951

It's the day after my birthday. I am one year older than yesterday, but feel more like ten years older. It's still bitter cold and windy, but the day is clear and sunny. The sun, however, isn't warm. Though I am sleepy and tired, I feel good. It's a good feeling knowing we obtained our objective. It's a better feeling knowing I made it through. Company G paid a high price for this hill. At this point no one knows how many men were killed or wounded. Losing one man is bad enough. I will never forget the night of my thirty-first birthday. Never! It still seems like a nightmare. As far as I'm concerned, Korea *is* a nightmare.

We are short of personnel. I am missing four men from the Second Platoon plus a squad leader and the wounded Lt. Grey. We need replacements. In order to regroup, to fill our vacancies, and merely to catch up on some rest, the Second Platoon is placed in reserve. We can wash up, shave, and generally clean up not only ourselves but our weapons and equipment too. Jammed or rusty rifles are useless. It's impossible to keep them clean and dry while on the move. But right now we all need a good, uninterrupted sleep and rest. Even if just for a short while.

I am given a letter from our regimental commander, Col. Harris, which lifts my spirits considerably. The letter is an acknowledgment of my birthday, February 14th. What a surprise!

February 18, 1951

This is the second day after another big battle. At approximately 11:00 AM, I witnessed a tragedy. A driver from the regimental motor pool drove past on a bulldozer, grading the road. (Road conditions are causing problems for our vehicles.) As he passed me, the bulldozer shovel hit a partially buried mine, causing it to explode. A piece

HEADQUARTERS 7TH CAVALRY REGIMENT
AFO 201

14 February 1951

SFC Boris Spiroff RA 6 894 579
Company G
7th Cavalry Regiment
AFO 201

Dear Sergeant Spiroff:

As records show that you have come to another anniversary marker in your life, I wish to extend you the congratulations and best wishes of the officers and men of the 7th Cavalry Regiment.

In these crucial instances of our lives, while away from our dear ones, and where we fight for the preservation of our beautiful ideals, it is with pleasure that I express an earnest desire for happy returns of the day, for your continuing success and for many happier occasions to come.

Sincerely,

W. A. HARRIS
Colonel, Arty
Commanding

Korea: Frozen Hell on Earth   51

of the metal flew up, striking the driver under his right eye. Soon the eye, blood, and parts of the brain began to emerge from the wound. The driver, in a state of shock, was still in a sitting position in the seat. Company medics, who were close by, carried him to the battalion aid station. There was no hope. He died shortly after. Another day starting wrong and we're not even in battle. I regret witnessing that and can't get it off my mind. Meanwhile, several new replacements arrive, but we are still under strength.

We receive notice that our rest period (reserve status) is over. We will be moving out, back on line, in the morning.

March 7, 1951

We are now at Hoengsong, arriving here after an eight day rest period. We had our breakfast of scrambled eggs with toast. It was a treat. The hot coffee is really enjoyable, speaking for myself. We hear that Gen. MacArthur with Gen. Ridgway will be visiting the Seventh Cavalry among other units that are in our sector. Our commanding officer does not know which battalion will be visited first, if any. They may just visit Col. Harris's command post at regimental headquarters. We are instructed to be on alert, look smart, and remain at our assigned positions. Everyone is to be clean-shaven and in proper uniform. No one is to be caught without a steel helmet! It is mandatory that we have steel helmets and that we shave whenever possible.

It's now 6:00 PM. The generals have departed without visiting Company G. Battalion has cautioned us to be on special alert during the night. Company F, four hundred yards to our front, informs that Chinese are attempting to infiltrate their perimeter. Two prisoners were captured in their area. I posted two listening posts in front of our perimeter, as did the First and Third Platoons. The night is getting pitch black and quiet. No one sleeps too soundly during the night, but luckily there are no visitors.

March 10, 1951

We have been here at Hoengsong for the past week. Today we are moving out on a search-and-destroy mission. Other than hearing the occasional crack of a sniper's rifle throughout the day, we encounter no major enemy group or stronghold, though we are in enemy territory. At dusk we turn in for the night, after securing our perimeter. Some of the men visit each other's positions, exchanging news from back home and showing pictures of family. I received a letter from Cassie containing her picture. I treasure it very much. It gives me inspiration and the desire to keep on.

March 11, 1951

We break camp after breakfast, March 11, and proceed to our next objective, the Han River area just east of Seoul. Before long we encounter several small unit actions with no major problems other than delaying action. Moving single file, a column on each side of a narrow road through a semi-cleared area, we are surprised by a sudden burst of fire, evidently from a hidden sniper.

I see Cpl. Riggs, my best squad leader, grab his chest and fall forward on his knees. He is approximately twenty yards to my right front. He is dead by the time I reach him, shot in the chest, never knowing what hit him. I feel terrible. He was only twenty-two years old, but a hell of a good squad leader. He wanted to meet my sister-in-law, Helen, upon returning home. He had already received a letter from her in answer to his.

Since I personally witnessed the incident, I must report to my commanding officer just how he was killed, in order to inform the family. This is one of the commanding officer's unpleasant duties. It's so depressing to see anyone killed, especially when he is close to you. It seems as if all the good ones go first! Korea is truly hell! (See letter to Cassie dated March 11, 1951.)

I asked Sgt. Link to select an acting squad leader. Cpl.

Riggs' incident is a double tragedy. Yesterday, he gave me two letters to mail for him, one to his mother and another to his sister. He told them that he would be due for rotation soon.

By mid afternoon we reach Han River and are successful in crossing it, occupying immediately the high ground. Everyone is wet, cold, and miserable from wading across. Walking in wet boots and socks is no picnic. I can't wait to remove them and change socks. After securing our position, it's late afternoon, and we take time out for our C-ration dinner. But first, a platoon latrine has to be dug (slit trench).

We turn in for the night after listening posts are in position. Between 10:00 and 11:00 PM, we are paid a visit by "Bed Check Charlie." It is a lone airplane of the enemy, flying in the dark, dropping cluster bombs on suspected UN positions. For making periodic flights during these hours, the pilot was given the name of Bed Check Charlie. Though this is only a harassing action, it is eerie hearing the plane overhead. All pray that the bombs do not fall in our area. Everyone is jumpy and sleep is disturbed.

March 14-15, 1951

Our drive keeps moving forward. We are meeting less and less resistance. At a briefing, our commanding officer informs us that the US Eighth Army is taking the offensive, full strength, against the Chinese/North Koreans occupying Seoul. This will be a major project and certainly no picnic. We are to move out, joining the main body of First Cavalry and head toward Seoul. This mission is named Operation Ripper.

All platoons are checked by the respective leaders, assuring each weapon is working properly and personnel have sufficient ammunition. We encounter bitter fighting along the way. Though casualties are occurring, we keep moving on. Artillery and mortar fire is preceding our advance, having an effect on the Chinese defenders. Many

White phosphorous support prior to assaulting
hill during Operation Ripper , March 14, 1951.

Chinese are bypassed. They are either surrendering or in a state of shock and confusion. Weakened by our superior firepower and approaching tanks, the Chinese are forced to give ground. They finally abandon Seoul. Once again Seoul is in our hands. More yo-yo warfare! Though many Chinese are killed, so are many civilians. Most of them were killed or tortured by the Chinese before they abandoned the city. Operation Ripper is a success, but at a price!

<u>March 18 - 20, 1951</u>

Having retaken Seoul, we move out to the surrounding high ground, where we stop for a two day rest period. We dig in, taking defensive positions around our perimeter in the event of a counter attack.

Today is Sunday. One good thing about being in a rest period or reserve status is that on Sundays religious services are available. Chaplains with assistants visit these areas, arriving in Jeeps. The services are held in open fields with the hoods of the Jeeps used as altars. Many men look forward to this. A group of us from Company G attended. It's so strange to see men receiving communion with rifles slung from their shoulders. I wonder if we are forgiven for breaking the commandment "Thou shall not kill"?

It is a nice sunny day and after service, we have a chance to clean up, wash, and shave. I appreciate my steel helmet, not so much for its safety purpose, which is why we are compelled to wear it, but for containing hot water for bathing and shaving purposes. We all need and appreciate the rest period. Today I was informed by my commanding officer that I was promoted to Master Sergeant effective March 10, which was eight days ago. This news really lifted my spirits considerably. It was a long time coming.

A short formation is held, attended by personnel available, announcing the promotion. I receive congratulations from the CO and the men. I wish there was some way to celebrate the promotion, to sort of "wet down the stripes" as on previous occasions when promoted.

March 23, 1951

The big news today is that airborne troops, for the first time, will be put into action. This mission, known as Operation Tomahawk, is for the airborne troops to jump at Munsan, supported by ranger units. There they will link up with a tank battalion and entrap a large North Korean encampment. This information was relayed to the platoon leaders and sergeants by Cap. Mulaison, our commanding officer. We are to move out in the morning.

March 31, 1951

For the past week our battalion has been constantly moving from one position to another. Walking in this terrain really wears you down, although we are all in good shape physically. Today we cleared an area two miles wide and almost as deep, but found no sign of the enemy. Everyone is exhausted and could use some rest. During the past four days Company G lost only one man, one of the recent arrivals assigned as BAR man of the heavy weapon squad. We reached Chunchon, near the Soyang River.

We received goods news. We are being relieved by the First Battalion, giving us a three-day rest. Some new replacements arrived today and were immediately assigned to squads short of personnel. We lost several men at the latest action around Seoul, in addition to those sent back earlier due to frostbite. Two were lost by stepping on personnel mines, which is another hazard.

Mines or mine fields are normally marked or deactivated by the mine-laying teams when the area is abandoned, if time and situation permit. Occasionally some mines are missed, thus becoming a hazard to everyone. Enemy mines, however, could be anywhere.

Meanwhile, a slit trench has to be dug for a latrine. This is necessary anytime a unit is in a reserve or rest status. A selected area is designated for either a company or platoon latrine. Squads take turns providing personnel. Latrines must be filled and marked when moving out.

Mail arrived today. I received two letters from Cassie and from family. Men receiving mail exchanged news from back home. This is one of the pleasantries, except for when heartbreaking letters are received informing one of a family member dying or being in an accident. This has happened on several occasions. Arrangements are made or requested for a chaplain's visit to give consolation, providing one is available. Then there are the "Dear John" letters, which are real morale breakers.

April 6, 1951

We have a platoon of ROK soldiers attached to Company G. They have proven to be good, well-trained soldiers. In spite of not being able to speak or understand English, except for their leader, they are very useful when clearing a village. They seem to be learning our tactics in fighting a limited war in this type of terrain. One thing we have learned about them is that they hate the North Koreans with a passion. The ROK soldiers do not like to take prisoners, believing all prisoners should be executed. The four North Korean prisoners that we had captured earlier were turned over to them to be delivered back to the division compound housing POWs. When they thought that they were out of our sight they made the prisoners kneel, then shot each one in the back of the head. This incident occurred when we were scattered in an open field eating our noon meal. I saw one of the prisoners stand up after being shot, take two steps forward, then fall face forward.

The ROK soldiers were admonished by our CO and warned not to do that ever again. A report of the incident was prepared and sent to battalion headquarters.

Battalion was aware that we had the prisoners and would safely deliver them to the compound at the first opportunity. (Some of the Chinese had leaflets in their possession, which had been dropped from planes, guaranteeing safe conduct should any soldier want to surrender. The leaflets, signed by Gen. MacArthur, were written in both English and Korean.)

April 9, 1951

We are in position, on line with other units, along "Line Kansas," just north of the Thirty-eighth parallel. At 3:00 PM, attending a critique, we were informed that the Chinese have partially opened the gates on the dam at Hwacchon Reservoir, flooding the Pukhan River. The river's overflow is causing a major problem for the Eighth Army's attack plans. The water rushing down stream flooded the terrain between IX Corps and the First Cavalry, nullifying the plans. It is imperative that the dam be captured, driving the Chinese away from it. This mission is given to Col. Calloway's Second Battalion, Seventh Cavalry. We are to move out in the morning. This will not be an easy task. The size and strength of the Chinese protecting the dam are undetermined. The First Marine Division is moving in now to temporarily assume our position on Line Kansas, freeing us for the objective. We turn in for the night.

April 10, 1951

We are up at 5:00 AM. After securing our equipment and checking our arms and ammunition, we eat a hearty breakfast of K-rations. We hit the trail by 6:30 AM. After a few miles our rapid advance is slowed considerably by the very hilly and rugged terrain. No vehicle larger than a Jeep can navigate the small, narrow roads. The 105 millimeter howitzers can't manage the roads to get near the dam. They will only be able to give limited support from long range. This is not good. Full power, close

These leaflets, signed by General Douglas McArthur
were dropped by aircraft on enemy positions guaranteeing
good treatment should they want to give up.

support, will be needed.

We are meeting enemy resistance along the way but are managing to advance through it. By nightfall we are within a half mile of the dam. Here we are halted, not being able to advance farther. The Chinese, in great numbers, are well dug-in and firing on us. They have the advantage in the line of fire, shooting down on us. It will be suicide to venture any farther, especially without the howitzers. We withdraw with no one killed and only minor casualties. The dam is left for another day and with more units involved. We move back to the Thirty-eighth parallel for bivouac and rest. It's getting dark and it looks and feels like it will rain before long. With God's blessing I survived another encounter, along with others.

April 11, 1951

We awoke to a very miserable and wet morning. Cold rain is running into our foxholes and bunkers, causing everyone to get up. It began raining about midnight as a light shower, gradually becoming heavier. The roads are a muddy mess. The vehicles are sliding into muddy ruts. However, there is one consolation. This type of rain is effecting the enemy as well. It's difficult for them to maneuver and sneak around as they like to do. With this heavy rain and wind even our ponchos are not helping too much, especially when we are all wet to start with. However, we would be lost without them.

We were just informed by Cap. Mulaison that President Truman has relieved Gen. MacArthur as Supreme Commander of the UN Forces. It is shocking news. There must be a reason for it. It likely will surface later. MacArthur's replacement is to be Gen. Matthew Ridgway. He only recently replaced Gen. Walker, Eighth Army Commander, who was killed.

The rain has subsided. We must move out, farther north from the Thirty-eighth parallel and deeper into enemy territory. Everyone is on edge, expecting something big to occur. At 6:00 PM we move up to the immediate high ground and dig in. We secure our perimeter in anticipation of a Chinese attack, but there is no sign of the enemy. Everyone breathes a sigh of relief, but we still feel jittery. The Seventh Cavalry is now in reserve with the entire First Cavalry Division. Col. Bill Harris is replaced by Colonel Dan Gilmer as Commanding Officer of the Seventh Cavalry.

April 14, 1951

This is our third day here. We are still in reserve, holding the ridge. There is still no sign of the enemy, but things are too quiet. The Chinese are up to something.

Being in reserve status, our mess personnel have moved up, providing us with hot meals. The scrambled eggs in the morning, though imitation, are a treat. I especially enjoy the hot coffee. The noon meal is okay too, providing one finds no fault with franks and beans. I can either take or leave the cornbread. We eat, dispersed from each other, one platoon at a time. Lt. Grey informs me that we will be moving out tomorrow morning up to Line Kansas. I informed the squad leaders. The rest period went by too fast!

We learned today that General Van Fleet has taken over the Eighth Army, replacing General Ridgway. The First Cavalry Division as well as all of the UN forces move farther up, taking positions along Line Kansas. It is north of Seoul and slightly north of the Thirty-eighth parallel, near Hwachan Reservoir.

Rumor is, according to G-2 information, that the Chinese are massing for a major offensive, determined to recapture Seoul. We are reminded to be on alert and ready for anything. Needless to say, everyone is jumpy and on edge, especially the new personnel. But when I say everyone, I mean everyone, including me. The men sleep for short periods of time, alternating with partners. They sleep with weapons in their hands. This is what makes the Korean War so exhausting—never any time for a good rest. There is rumbling of artillery fire in the distance. Someone else is not sleeping.

April 20 - 30, 1951

The quiet is over. The Chinese are on the move and have begun their attack. Hundreds of them are right in front of our sector. They are coming down from the hills facing us, advancing through the valley, approaching the foot of our hill. This is hard to believe. They are easy targets from our advantageous position, but there are too many of them. They are swarming in from all directions, climbing over their dead, with more coming down the hill. This is forcing us to fall back even though they are only armed mostly with small weapons, grenades and mortars. As they come forward they are yelling, screaming, whistling and blowing bugles. They seen to be in a trance, some turning around after being shot, going the opposite way.

Being in front of the main line, our battalion retreats to Line Kansas and falls into position. We are now getting heavy firepower support. Artillery and mortar fire is taking a toll on the Chinese. They are unable to penetrate our defenses and are stopped short of the Han River and Seoul. They suffered many, many casualties. Men in brown quilted uniforms can be seen everywhere. We also have our share of casualties and will need to reorganize as soon as possible. The main thing is they did not retake Seoul.

We dig in, establishing a perimeter, and wait, either for the enemy to strike or for moving-out orders from regimental headquarters.

May 4 - June 4, 1951

During the past five or six weeks it's been up and down from one position to the next. Even without any fire fight, coping with this terrain is a struggle. Especially when the heavy rains of spring come down in torrents. The ponchos are of little help in keeping us dry, but are helpful as windbreakers. We are now holding Line Lincoln along Uijongbu Road, assisting the U.S. Sixty-fourth Tank Battalion.

There is a rumor all along the line that peace negotiations are soon to take place. This rumor is giving everyone hope that the fighting will end and all troops will be home for Christmas. Many men are actually joyous, anticipating a trip home soon. However, there is still fighting going on north of us, around Charwon and the Kwacchon Reservoir. Any cease-fire in the near future is only wishful thinking. After some bitter fighting and many casualties on both sides, Charwon is taken by the U.S. Third and Twenty-Fifth Divisions.

Company G is authorized to send four men for a five day R and R in Japan. One man is from my platoon. Personnel eligible are the ones in Korea longest. They will return after five days. However, two of them are soon to be sent to Headquarters upon their return. They have accumulated enough points for rotation back to the States. They are among the lucky ones that have survived this hell hole. I am glad for them.

July 10, 1951

The long awaited peace negotiations are finally in progress. A so called armistice was announced on June 23. A cease-fire was agreed on with the negotiations to begin today, July 10, at Kaesong. We are at Yonchon, to the left of the Third Infantry Division, along the UN line.

Everyone seems to be in great hopes, thinking that the beginning of the war's end has arrived. But no such luck! Even with the negotiations in progress, minor patrol battles and skirmishes are taking place. Each side is attempting to seize key hill and terrain positions, particularly OPs. This is in the event the negotiations break down. Men are leery and nervous about going on patrols now. No one wants to get killed or seriously

Somewhere in Korea. Ready for
a shave—all I need is some water.

wounded when the time for returning home is so close.

We are paid another visit by Bed Check Charlie. Another night's sleep is disturbed and everyone is jittery. Luckily, there are no hits on our position.

July 15, 1951

Finally my turn has come. I was just informed by Lt. Grey, who has returned to duty, to prepare myself for a five day R and R trip to Japan. This is the best news I have received since being informed of my promotion. It will be good to get away from combat, even for just a little while. I lose no time in getting ready. I can hardly wait for a nice hot bath.

I arrive in Japan in good order, the weather and trip being fine and pleasant. I plan to take in some sights, buy some souvenirs, and eat some Class A food for a change. I have my mind set on a chocolate sundae for desert, but first, the long awaited hot bath then a gift for Cassie. I have a chance to have my stripes sewn on my uniform.

I called Cassie and the connection was good. She was so surprised to hear from me. It was so good to hear her voice. Later on I decided to try a rickshaw ride. I feel sorry for the person pulling the rickshaw, but I enjoy the ride. Regretfully, my time is up. The five days have gone so fast. I hate to return to Korea, but . . .

July 22, 1951

I returned to my unit today. Even before I can relax from my trip the company has to move out on a probing mission. I was hoping that during the R and R stay the peace negotiations would have eased our situation. But no such luck. Hostilities are continuing during the talks. We keep moving from one hill to another, from one ridge to another, from one high ground to one still higher. We don't have any fat people in Company G anymore. In fact, when I arrived in Korea I weighed 170 pounds. I now weigh less than 150.

Lunching at the USO Club. (I'm having a long awaited milk shake.)

July 1951. Tokyo, Japan. On five day R and R (the shortest five days in my memory). I hated the thought of returning to my unit, but . . .

Today we encountered some resistance in climbing a rocky mountain to reach our objectives. We were successful in dislodging the Chinese and North Koreans without any casualties. Another strategic hill in our hands. If I ever return home, I won't care if I never see another hill.

We have moved up, near Charwon. Defending Charwon, facing us, is a strong Chinese unit according to G-2 reports. Our objective is to take Charwon.

August 10 - 15, 1951

The Second Battalion is deployed along the high ground here at Charwon, which we have recently taken more easily than we anticipated. Company G is the forward company responsible for the battalion's frontal perimeter. I am scheduled to take out a reconnaissance patrol around the perimeter at 5:00 PM. I informed the twelve persons detailed for the patrol to meet me at 4:00 PM for a final briefing and equipment check. Everyone returns to his squad or assigned position until briefing time.

Meanwhile, the peace negotiations, we are told, have hit a snag. During the negotiations on July 30, Marine aircraft bombed Pyongyang, inflicting much damage to the North Korean capitol. There seems to be a disagreement between the two sides on where the Thirty-eighth parallel should be. Though the negotiations are in progress, here on line it is business as usual.

At 4:00 PM, while checking out the patrol, outlining our mission and giving a final briefing, my platoon leader, Lt. Grey, informs me that Sergeant Smith is to replace me. Sergeant Smith is to take the patrol out. The reason for the switch is because the word came down from headquarters that I have accumulated the required points for rotation. My orders from battalion are to pack up my belongings immediately and report to headquarters for processing. I am both shocked at the news and elated.

However, I have been anticipating this for some time, knowing that I was close to having the required points.

This course of events has made me very happy, to say the least, but I hate leaving my platoon. I have great fondness for all the men and an admiration for Company G in general. We have been through a lot and have gained a lot of respect for one another.

SFC William Link, my assistant, will take over the Second Platoon. I am glad for him. He is a very good, sharp soldier with over five years of service. I wish the platoon the best of luck, an end to the war, and an eventual safe return home. My parting words to Lt. Grey, who was wounded on Hill 578, are: "Lieutenant Grey, I hope your promotion to captain comes soon—you deserve it—but above all, you'd better learn how to dodge!" Laughingly he agrees and wishes me a safe return home.

August 16 - 18, 1951

I arrived today, August 16, at battalion headquarters for the initial processing. From here I will go to regimental headquarters to fill out additional forms prior to moving to division headquarters. From there I will officially depart the First Cavalry Division.

Today, August 17, I am at regimental headquarters. During my processing, I receive disheartening news. I was informed that Sergeant Smith, who replaced me taking out the reconnaissance patrol, was killed by enemy mortar fire while on patrol.

Fortunately, none of the other members were hit, evidently being well dispersed. I feel terrible. He was a young man who had plans for making the army his career if he survived the war. He deserved a much better fate. What makes it worse and hurts so much more is that it was my patrol that he took out. It is difficult to describe just how I feel. Korea is truly hell. Even on my leaving the war, I learn of yet another senseless killing of a friend and fellow soldier.

We, myself and a few others from the cavalry, are now at division headquarters. We are awaiting the arrival of more personnel with the required points prior to moving to Inchon, a seaport on the west coast of Korea. It will be our final holding area prior to shipment.

September 10, 1951

Today we arrived at Inchon. We are staying in a barbed wire enclosed compound until the arrival of our ship. This place resembles a prison yard, evidently being a former POW compound. The area, however, is pleasant with adequate sleeping quarters. The personnel running the camp are very friendly and hospitable. I cannot find fault with the food. After existing on K- and C- rations for the past year, anything would be an improvement. The food and the cooks are exceptional. It's a pleasure to sit down and eat three meals a day without worrying who or what is behind each bush and tree. Throughout the day we are listening to stateside music. Three of the hottest new singers are Patti Page, Guy Mitchell, and Tony Bennett. Last night we saw our first movie in a long time. It was a musical comedy starring Jerry Lewis and Dean Martin, a new comedy team. Jerry Lewis's antics are enough to take a person's mind off the fighting.

I finally got the ham and egg breakfast that I longed for not too long ago. Not did I get it only once, but I have it each morning.

September 23, 1951

After almost two weeks of waiting, our ship finally arrived. Most of the men are packed and ready to board almost immediately, even before breakfast. However, breakfast is served and following it we board ship at 10:00 AM. The ship's anchor is raised and we pull out at 12:00 noon, bound for the good old U.S.A. Hooray!

While boarding the ship we heard over the loudspeaker system that back at the front fighting was continuing. The First Marine Division and the U.S. Second Division are in a bloody battle at Heartbreak Ridge. I wish them luck and victory! When will the fighting end?

As we pull out, the waters of Osan Bay, leading to the Yellow Sea, are rough and choppy even in the harbor. Nothing about Korea is pleasant.

After several hours of sailing, we hit some rough going. Many on board are becoming seasick, including me. To me it seems as though the Pacific Ocean is much rougher than the Atlantic.

There are approximately six hundred personnel on board, all coming from various units. I ran into Sergeant Pondish, from the Twenty-fourth Infantry, who was the mess sergeant of Company L, Fourteenth Infantry, when I was in Panama from 1937 to 1940. I also ran into Sergeant Vanadore who was my platoon sergeant during the same period. We had a lot to talk about, reliving old memories of better times. Approximately half way home we listened to the final game of the National League playoffs between the New York Giants and the Brooklyn Dodgers on the shortwave radio. Each team has won three games. In this, the seventh of the series, the score is tied in the last half of the ninth inning. With two outs, Bobby Thompson of the Giants hit a home run. The announcer screamed that it was a "shot heard around the world!" And he was right. We heard it half way around the world. The Giants won the right to play the American League champions in the World Series.

Though I am happy to be returning home, thankfully being among those who survived a hellish war, I don't feel exactly elated. I don't see faces here, among so many unfamiliar faces, that should be on their way home with me. Of the twelve men who left Fort Meade when I did, there are only three left, including me. The others have been either killed, wounded, captured, or are just missing. Perhaps some are still fighting, waiting for their turn for rotation.

We must never forget that many won't be coming home. Each has given his all for his country and for freedom. Wherever they are, our prayers should be for them. For those that are gone, may their souls rest in peace.

October 7, 1951

We docked today in Seattle, Washington, arriving by bus at Camp Lawson. The trip from Korea took fourteen days. It's great to be back on land again, and it will take a while to get rid of my "sea legs." It still feels as if I'm on deck. The weather is wet and foggy, reminding me so much of the weather in London, England, and of the early morning weather in Scotland, with fog remaining for most of the mornings.

I called Cassie and it was so good hearing her voice. She was so surprised to hear from me, and surprised we were in Washington and that the trip took so long. I can hardly wait to get home. There is still some processing we must go through.

October 8 - 10, 1951

Arrived at Friendship, Maryland at 8:00 PM by way of Chicago. Instead of reporting to Fort Meade, I took a taxi home to Linthicum, surprising Cassie with my unexpected arrival. I don't know who was more thrilled to see the other. I will spend the night here at home and report to Fort Meade in the morning.

The following morning, while waiting for the Fort Meade bus, I was offered a ride to Fort Meade by Warrant Officer Hammond, who was on the way there. He told me that my former unit, the Third Armored Cavalry Regiment, had shipped out of Fort Meade.

I reported to Personnel with great anxiety, for I did not know where my next assignment would be. I still had eighteen months remaining of my three-year enlistment when I joined the Third Cavalry. I was in hopes of rejoining them and seeing my former commanding officer, Captain James McAloon, a very sharp officer, as well as seeing the old soldier, First Sergeant MacDonald. I especially wanted to get reacquainted with my old friends and buddies,

Sergeants Schwartz and Jantzen, both old soldiers and model NCOs. Bill Schwartz taught me all I know about tank warfare, tank maneuvers, and the care and maintenance of the tanks and personnel carriers during the six months prior to my departure for Korea. Sergeant Jantzen, the unit's communication sergeant, taught all of us the proper method of communication between tank commanders as well as tank commanders with ground troops. He was one of the finest radio and telephone specialists I have known. The three of us spent many pleasant working hours between Fort Meade and A. P. Hill, Virginia. I learned that several platoon members were sent to Korea after my departure, one being Corporal Hart, who was KIA. Another good friend lost!

Since the Cavalry moved out, I am hoping for an assignment close to home. Once more luck is with me. I am assigned as a Regular Army Instructor for the 175th Infantry Regiment, Maryland National Guard, Baltimore, Maryland. I am the instructor for the Second Battalion. Master Sergeant Alex Berg has the First Battalion, while Master Sergeant D. Waddington has the Third. We all report to chief instructor Major W. DeVos.

With this assignment I feel as though I am on "cloud nine." I cannot believe it. Cassie is so happy and thrilled. An assignment such as this is given only to a select few and is commonly known in army terms as a "gravy assignment."

To get closer to my assigned station, Cassie and I have moved from Linthicum to an apartment in Baltimore. We are only a few miles from the Armory. We are staying with Bud and Nadine Engler. We would soon become the best of friends.

Meanwhile, it appears that the peace negotiations in Korea have been put on hold, temporarily discontinued, due to minor disagreements. Minor skirmishes and patrol actions between the two sides are still continuing along the Thirty-eighth parallel. Casualties keep mounting.

Received photo of Cassie on March 10, 1951
while in reserve status at Hoengsang.

Back from Korea, November 1951, with Cassie and aunt.

M. Sgt. Boris Spiroff receiving the Bronze Star from Lt. Col. John D. Underwood for heroism in action in Korea, October 1950.

Sgt. Spiroff Wins Award For Valor

M/Sgt. Boris Spiroff has re-ceived the Oak Leaf Cluster to his Bronze Star Medal with "V" (for valor) device for gallantry in ac-tion in Korea.

His wife, Mrs. Catherine Spiroff, lives at 1716 Dukeland street.

Spiroff was cited for heroism while forming and leading an as-sault group which routed the en-emy near Paiu-ri.

Korea: Frozen Hell on Earth

Newspaper headlines and news on radio and television are not too encouraging.

November 27, 1951

I have been home almost two months. We have just returned from a week of maneuvers at A. P. Hill, Virginia. Here we faced more inclement weather, muddy fields, combat conditions and eating in the field, but it was a pleasure. No one got shot or even slightly injured. The hardest part was cleaning up the equipment and vehicles!

The big news today, November 27, is that peace negotiations have been reestablished. The talks are to resume in the city of Panmunjon. Today should have marked the end of all hostilities and offensive action in Korea. But sadly it didn't. Though the truce talks are in progress, the final end of the war is still not in sight. As of this date, fighting in Korea is still going on and the casualties continue to mount.

This marks the end of my personal involvement and experience during my Korea tenure. I cannot comment on any further Korean action or development. I must rely on what is printed or broadcast in the daily news. This also marks the end of my Korea timetable.

America should have learned one important lesson from this Korea venture. That is to never again get involved in another nation's problems at the expense of American lives. It's too high of a price to pay!

APPROXIMATE COUNT OF THE KOREAN WAR
(POLICE ACTION)
As of December, 1951:
Killed .... Over 40,000
Wounded .... Over 105,000
Missing or POWS .... Exact number unknown, estimated to be in the thousands

(See Epilogue for final count of the Korean War.)

Appendix 1

General Order #228, 20 August 1951, Section II

<u>AWARD OF THE BRONZE STAR MEDAL</u>
Oak Leaf Cluster

By direction of the President, under the provisions of Executive Order 9415, 4 February 1944 (Section II, W D Bul 3, 1944), and pursuant to authority contained in AR 600-5, the Bronze Star Medal (First Oak Leaf Cluster) with "V" Device for heroic achievement in connection with military operations against an enemy of the United States is awarded to the following enlisted man:
Master Sergeant BORIS SPIROFF (then Sergeant First Class) RA 689-4579, Infantry, United States Army, Company G, 7th Cavalry Regiment, 1st Cavalry Division, for heroism in action against the enemy on October 15, 1950, near Paiu-Ri, Korea. As Company G advanced toward the objective, they were suddenly pinned down by intense enemy mortar and machine gun fire. Sergeant SPIROFF, aware of the extreme danger confronting the company, formed an assault group of two squads from his platoon. Disregarding his personal safety, he led the men across an open area under a hail of deadly fire to high ground, where he skillfully deployed his men and formed a surprise attack on the enemy flank. By destroying several machine gun emplacements and forcing the foe to flee in great disorder, the assault force enabled the remainder of the company to move on toward the objective. Sergeant SPIROFF's heroism reflects great credit on himself and the military service.

Entered federal service from Maryland.

Appendix 2

FIRST CAVALRY DIVISION'S
KOREAN WAR CAMPAIGNS

UN Defensive .... June 1950

UN Offensive .... June - November 1950

Chinese Forces
(CCF Intervention) .... December 1950

First UN Counter
Offensive .... January - March 1951

Chinese Communist
Spring Offensive .... May 1951

UN Summer - Fall
Offensive .... July - September 1951

Second Korean Winter .... November 1951

Bibliography

The Korea War. General Matthew B. Ridgway. Garden City, New York: Doubleday, 1967.

The Forgotten War. Clay Blair (Times Books). New York: Doubleday, 1987.

To The Yalu. J. McGovern. New York: Morrow Books, 1972.

Korea War. Stephan Badsey. New York: Gallery Books, 1990.

Epilogue

September 19, 1994

Today marks the forty-third anniversary of my leaving Korea. I have concluded a manuscript of my year in Korea during the war—thus ending my diary. Though I returned home in October 1951, the war had not ceased. The peace negotiations, which began in July 1951, were still in progress, continuing for another sixteen months. Peace was finally declared on March 27, 1953. Major frontline battles had subsided during the negotiations, but skirmishes by small unit patrols for strategic hills and areas continued, raising the casualty count by 14,000 killed, 17,000 wounded, and approximately 8,000 missing. This brought the final casualty count to 54,500 killed, 103,300 wounded and 8,000 plus missing. What a waste of human life! And for what?! It is now forty-three years later, and trouble between the North and South is again brewing.

Though I lost contact with the Cavalry after my return, I continued my army career. Following the National Guard assignment (mentioned at the close of my book), I was assigned to the Sixteenth Infantry Regiment, First Army Division, Stuttgart, Germany. In December 1954, on returning from Germany, I was assigned as First Sergeant of Battery A, First Battalion, Eighty-ninth Artillery, Fort Meade, Maryland. (On August 28, 1955, a major event in my life occurred when my son, John, was born.)

From 1955 to 1962, I remained in the Artillery as First

Sergeant of various batteries within the Thirty-fifth AAA Brigade. I retired in August 1962 from Headquarters and Headquarters Battery, 562nd Missile Battalion, Fort Meade, Maryland, with twenty-five years of service.

In August 1958, at the Army Chemical Center, Edgewood, Maryland, I earned my two year (GED) college level degree. In October 1962, I was employed by Westinghouse Electric Corporation. I retired in January 1991, a year after my wife died of cancer.

My army career has been hectic and interesting, being stationed in many parts of the world and lucky to have survived two major wars. Unfortunately, thousands never made it. They lie, buried in foreign soil throughout the world. It is my fervent hope that we, America, will have learned a lesson about getting involved in another nation's problems, especially without provocation. We have paid a high enough price for an elusive peace!

Index of Significant Dates

Spiroff